# The Agile Self-assessment Game

## An Agile Coaching Tool for Improving the Agility of Your Teams and Organization

Ben Linders

This book is for sale at http://leanpub.com/self-assessment

This version was published on 2020-09-07

ISBN 978-94-92119-16-2

Leanpub

This is a Leanpub book. Leanpub empowers authors and publishers with the Lean Publishing process. Lean Publishing is the act of publishing an in-progress ebook using lightweight tools and many iterations to get reader feedback, pivot until you have the right book and build traction once you do.

# Tweet This Book!

Please help Ben Linders by spreading the word about this book on Twitter!

The suggested tweet for this book is:

I'm reading The Agile Self-assessment Game: An Agile Coaching Tool for Improving the Agility of Your Teams and Organization #AssessAgility

The suggested hashtag for this book is #AssessAgility.

Find out what other people are saying about the book by clicking on this link to search for this hashtag on Twitter:

#AssessAgility

# Also By Ben Linders

What Drives Quality

Getting Value out of Agile Retrospectives

Waardevolle Agile Retrospectives

Welchen Wert Agile Retrospektiven liefern

Tirer profit des rétrospectives agiles

Obtendo Valor de Retrospectivas Ágeis

Ottieni il meglio dalle tue Retrospettive Agili

Извлекаем пользу из Agile-ретроспектив

Obteniendo valor de las Retrospectivas ágiles

从敏捷回顾中收获价值

アジャイルふりかえりから価値を生み出す – 日本語版

Wartościowe Retrospekcje Agile

Continuous Improvement

Αποκομίζοντας αξία από τα Agile Retrospectives

Khai thác giá trị Agile Retrospective

Jak zvýšit přínos agilních retrospektiv

Problem? What Problem?

Agile Manifesto Retrospectives Questions Cards

Agile Testing Coaching Cards

Agile Retrospectives Bingo

Agile Retrospective Smells Cards

*This book is dedicated to all the great agile teams around the world to help them become even better!*

*The game plays through quite easily and participants remarked that the exercise was quite valuable. We generated a ton of insights and even some concrete action items (which is relatively rare for this team).*

Craig Eddy, Chief Developer at Empact Development


*It's a great tool to use for a retrospective. The game engages the whole team and generates good discussion.*

Christine Schubert, Agile Coach at National Council of Architectural Registration Boards


*I have played the agile self-assessment with multiple teams. The participants had little experience with (serious) games, but the game was self-explaining and the teams had great fun playing. As the agile self-assessment is played in low threshold manner, I would recommend it for every team that is struggling with improving the agile process.*

Berry Kersten, Agile consultant at Improve Quality Services


*I really recommend the Self Assessment Game for Scrum Masters or Agile Teams as a way to facilitate and focus the discussion about possible improvements.*

Andreas Schliep, Executive Partner at DasScrumTeam


*The Agile Self-Assessment Game helped us to reflect on where we are in a fun way.*

Peter Rubarth, Scrum Master, Agile Coach & Master Produceer

# Contents

# Preface

I'm an active blogger at www.benlinders.com. On my blog, I share my experiences on agile and lean topics, including agile self-assessments.

I have always been a big fan of assessments. They help you to reflect, see how you are doing, and find ways to improve.

In the early nineties, I started doing assessments with the Capability Maturity Model (CMM) which later became the CMMI. I preferred doing class C assessments; focused mini-assessments where I worked intensively together with professionals to help them find out how well they were doing and what they could improve on.

When agile started taking off in this century, many of teams that I worked with wanted to find out how agile they are. I searched for tools and checklists on agile which I studied in detail. I also tried out some of them, where I tailored them to suit the specific needs of the teams/organizations that I work with.

Over the years I found many checklists and tools that can be used for self-assessment; I'm listing them on my Agile Self-Assessment Tools and Checklists webpage which I'm maintaining since September 2013.

Early 2016 I created the first version of my card game to do Agile Self-assessments with teams. I started using the game more often in my workshops to teach agile practices and when I coach teams to help them reflect and improve at their own pace. Every time I used it I adapted the game by improving the statements on the cards, dropping cards, and adding new cards.

The first public appearance with the Agile Self-assessment Game was at XP Days 2016. The room was fully booked, people really liked the game and spoke highly of it.

Next, I added the game to my webshop. In the first months, 1000++ people downloaded the game and played it. It got great reviews and became a big success. I added expansion packs for specific agile frameworks and updated the game based on the feedback received and my experiences from playing it.

This is the first book specifically about Agile Self-assessments. In this book, I explain what self-assessments are and why you would do them, and explore how to do them using the Agile Self-assessment Game. I'm also sharing experience stories from people who played the game.

This book is based on my experience as a developer, tester, team leader, project manager, quality manager, process manager, consultant, coach, trainer, and adviser in Agile, Lean, Quality and Continuous Improvement. It takes a deep dive into self-assessments, viewing them from different perspectives and provides ideas, suggestions, practices, and experiences that will help you to do effective agile self-assessments with your teams.

I'm aiming this book at Scrum masters, agile coaches, consultants leading agile transformations, developers and testers, project managers, line managers, and CxOs; basically for anyone who is looking for an effective way to help their agile teams improve and to increase the agility of their organization.

I love to hear your experiences from playing the game. Feel free to email me at benlinders@gmail.com!

Finally, I would like to thank all the people who invest time to read my blog and comment on the articles. Your feedback helps me to increase my understanding of the topics that I write about and makes it worthwhile for me to keep blogging!

Ben Linders
January 2019

# Introduction

This book is about Agile Self-assessments, a practice that teams and organizations use to explore how well they are doing and come up with ideas to improve their agility.

**What's in This Book**

In this book, I explore the Agile Self-assessment Game, a card game that I created and that is now played by teams all over the world. Teams use it to reflect on their own interworking and to agree upon the next steps for their agile journey.

There's a full chapter with Playing Suggestions which provides ideas for how to play the game in your teams.

I'm providing Experience Stories, from myself and from others who played the game, to inspire you and share how to use the cards and show what the game can do.

The list of Frequently Asked Questions provide answers to any question that you might have about agile self-assessments and playing the game.

The Agile Self-assessment Game is one of the ways to assess your agility. The chapter Assessment Tools and Checklists provides additional checklists and tools for agile assessments.

This *Agile Self-assessments* book doesn't intend to teach you the theory behind self-assessments or provide detailed descriptions of all possible self-assessment tools and practices. There are several possibilities to get training and support for playing the game.

The Bibliography provides an extensive list of books, articles, and links, that you can use to acquire in-depth knowledge of self-assessments.

## How To Use the Book

This is a practical book with many techniques and ideas that you can apply in your specific situation. It aims to help you to support teams that want to improve and become fully self-organized.

There are many suggestions in this book which help you to apply self-assessments. They are marked as tips with a key symbol:

 Try those tips that look suitable and see if they work for you. If they do, great! If not, try another one.

I also added stories and cases from organizations that I have worked with to share my experience:

 Stories and cases are boxed with a user symbol. Use them to get inspiration and think about what you might do.

The suggestions provided in this book are suitable for agile coaches, Scrum masters, agile teams, and managers of agile organizations.

 Register your book today to get access to supporting materials and download the card decks for playing games from this book with a discount at benlinders.com/agile-self-assessment-game.

With plenty of ideas, suggestions, and practical cases on Agile Self-assessments, this book will help you to apply assessments in your organization and help teams to improve.

# Agile Self-assessment Game

The Agile Self-Assessment Game is used by teams and organizations to self-assess their agility. Playing the game enables teams to reflect on their own team interworking and agree upon the next steps for their agile journey.

With this card game, teams and organizations can discover how agile they are and what they can do to increase their agility to deliver more value to their customers and stakeholders.

In this chapter, I explore what you can do to assess your agility and explain how the Agile Self-assessment Game can be used to do assessments and support improvements.

# Assessing your Agility

Agile methods and frameworks like Scrum, Kanban, SAFe or LeSS, don't tell you how to increase your agility. They provide practices, roles, and activities, and a structure which fits them together. But they are not recipes that can help you to truly become agile.

 The values and principles from the manifesto for agile software development state that you have to find your own way for becoming agile, by reflecting how you are doing and finding out where and how you need to improve.

An agile self-assessment is a technique to find out how agile you are. Such assessments are normally done by the teams themselves, by investigating their way of working against the agile mindset, principles, and practices.

Self-assessments can be question-based or they can use checklists or frameworks to assess team performance. They can be used to investigate and discuss the use of agile practices and techniques and evaluate their contribution towards the value that is being delivered by teams.

 Agile teams use self-assessments to find out how well they are performing.

Teams can use agile self-assessments to decide what practices they want to use and how to apply them in a way that helps them to do their work efficiently and effectively.

As the name suggests, agile self-assessments are the kind of assessment that professional team members can and should do themselves. This is what makes them different from external assessments or audits.

With agile self-assessments, teams are free to decide what to do and how to do it. Neither the assessment nor the results are imposed on the team.

Self-assessment can help you to increase the agility of your organization.

 Agile coaches and consultants use self-assessments in agile transformations to guide teams and help them learn about agile to find their own way.

# Gamification

The self-assessment practices (the game and playing suggestions) described in this book are based on gamification. Gamification is an approach where principles and practices from gaming are used in a non-gaming context.

In my work, I apply gamification in a business and team working context. It's about using practices from gaming to support professionals that are working together to deliver more business value; adding game aspects to their daily work to enable change and foster continuous sustainable improvement.

 My experience is that gamification is a great way to engage and involve people.

There are significant differences between games and gamification. The main ones are:

- Games are normally used to learn new things and to practice them, where gamification intents to inspire people and encourage behavior change.
- Gamification focuses on the intended outcome and the results, where games give attention to the rules and the processes.

Both games and gamification have value, but when it comes to self-assessments and organizational change I prefer to use gamification as it gets people involved in their own agile journey.

Although I'm applying gamification, I decided to use the term "game" for the assessment approach described in this book. Games appeal to people and are something they are often willing to try out. If the term "game" confuses people in your situation and context, feel free to use "gamification" or use another term that works for you.

The Agile Self-assessment Game explored in this book is not meant to be a game in the strict sense of the word where people have to play it "by the rules" and where there are winners and losers. Actually, with most of playing suggestions described in this book, everyone wins the game if they share and collaborate. There are no losers :-).

 Where many games have winners and losers, I prefer to play games in such a way that people never feel like if they have "lost the game". For me, winning is not the main objective to have people play games, it's sharing, learning, and initiating change that I want to aim at.

The benefits that I have seen from using gamification in Agile Self-assessments are:

- People like to play games, it brings out their natural desires to socialize, self-express, and collaborate
- Gamification provides a different perspective and culture, which leads to new valuable insights
- Playing games with teams stimulates collaboration and helps to build relationships
- Gamification is a way to visualize what's happening which helps people to align and decide
- You can create an environment with gamification where people feel safe to speak up and be open and honest

The Agile Self-assessment Game is a gamified approach for reflection and learning. It's a behavioral game that helps to initiate and reinforce positive behavioral change by people in organizations.

# Playing the Game

The Agile Self-assessment Game is played with decks of coaching cards specifically developed for this game. The cards contain statements that describe agile values, principles, and practices.

Examples of such statements are:

- The team is committed and takes responsibility for delivery
- Impediments are raised, recorded and resolved in a timely fashion
- The daily stand-up focuses on ongoing work, work that needs to be done, and impediments, and lasts no more than 15 minutes

**Cards printouts**

There are many ways to play games with these cards. This book provides you with Playing Suggestions; sample games and gamification techniques for using the cards depending on the situation at hand and the goal that you want to reach.

You can use the playing suggestions in this book for chartering teams, assessing performance, or as exercises in your agile retrospectives.

The game can also be played at a meetup, games night or in an open space, in a coaching retreat or agile coach camp, or at any other occasion where you want to learn from each other and have some fun.

# Getting the Cards

The basic Agile Self-Assessment Cards deck has 52 cards with statements on applying agile principles and practices. These cards can be downloaded in PDF format in my Agile Games webshop.

Expansion packs with additional cards are also available in the webshop. These packs contain cards with statements covering specific principles and practices from agile methods and frameworks.

 I highly recommended using one or more of the expansion packs when doing self-assessments in your organization, based of the methods and frameworks that the organization has adopted.

Currently, the following expansion packs are available:

- Scrum
- DevOps
- Busines Agility
- Kanban

Agile Self-assessment Cards are available in multiple languages:

- Agile Self-assessment Game - English
- Juego Autoevaluación Ágil - Spanish Edition
- Agilní sebehodnotící hra - Czech edition
- Gra Agile Self-Assessment - Polish edition
- Agile Zelfevaluatie Kaarten - Dutch edition
- Jeu de cartes d'autoévaluation Agile - French edition

 Support the developer of the game and get Free Lifetime Support by downloading your games and expansion packs directly from BenLinders.com!

The book with cards is published through Leanpub. Multiple languages are supported with specific packages, currently available are:

Agile Self-assessment Game - English edition: The book (in English) with the main Agile cards and expansions packs for Scrum, Kanban, DevOps, and Business Agility.

Juego Autoevaluación Ágil - Spanish edition: The book (in English) with the main Agile cards in Spanish and expansions packs in Spanish for Scrum, Kanban, DevOps, and Business Agility.

Agilní sebehodnotící hra - Czech edition: The book (in English) with the main Agile cards in Czech and expansions packs in Czech for Scrum,, Kanban, DevOps, and Business Agility.

Gra Agile Self-Assessment - Polish edition: The book (in English) with the main Agile cards in Polish and expansions packs in Polish for Scrum, DevOps, and Business Agility.

Agile Zelfevaluatie Kaarten - Dutch edition: The book (in English) with the main Agile cards in Dutch and expansions packs in Dutch for Scrum, Kanban, and DevOps.

Jeu de cartes d'autoévaluation Agile - French edition: The book (in English) with the Agile cards in French.

Find more information about the above packages (book and cards) here.

Summing up: Did you buy the book without cards, or do you want to extend your existing game with cards in another language? Here's how you can get the cards for playing the games described in this book:

 Visit my Agile Games Webshop to download decks of cards in your preferred language or extend your game with expansion packs.

or

 Register your book and buy card decks with a discount at benlinders.com/agile-self-assessment-game!

The Agile Self-assessment Game, the cards, and all Expansion Packs are licensed under a CC BY-NC-ND 3.0 License. If you want to use the game commercially, please contact Ben Linders.

# Doing Retrospectives using Assessments

Agile retrospectives are a great way for the teams to inspect and adapt their way of working. I highly recommend them, my first book Getting Value out of Agile Retrospectives and the Retrospective Exercises Toolbox provide many exercises that you can use to keep your retrospectives valuable.

Normally retrospectives look at the past iteration/sprint to define actions for the next one. This makes them useful to address issues that teams are dealing with currently, but less suitable to guide the teams' agile journey and to keep your agile transformation on track. For that, you need a tool that tells you where you are and where to go next. This is where agile self-assessments fit in.

 You can play the Agile Self-assessment Game in your retrospective to guide your agile journey and increase agility.

The game can be used in retrospectives for teams that have recently started; they can check which practices to pick up in next sprints.

It's also suitable for experienced teams where team members are already are well adapted to each other, to search for new improvements for their team working.

# Playing Suggestions

If you want to become more Agile and Lean, my recommendation is to frequently assess how you are doing by playing games using the Agile Self-assessment Game.

Before you can play a game you need to create the cards. Detailed instructions are included in this chapter for doing that.

There are many different ways to play the Agile Self-assessment Game. This chapter provides you with a variety of playing suggestions.

 You can use these suggestions to play the game or to design your own playing format.

I love to hear how you played the Agile Self-assessment Game! Feel free to send an email with the playing suggestion that you used and how that worked out for you to benlinders@gmail.com.

# Creating the Cards

The cards for the Agile Self-assessment Game are distributed in PDF format. There are 9 cards on each A4 page where all cards have the same size (70 mm by 99 mm). The cards are equally spaced.

To create the cards for the game, download the game and print the PDF files. Depending on your expected usage and your printer possibilities, you can print cards on normal copier paper (80 g/m2), heavier paper, or on photo paper.

 You might laminate the cards if you intend to use them frequently.

 Note that the cards are in "A4" format and not in "Letter". If you want to use paper in letter size, my suggestion would be to scale the A4 page while keeping hight and width proportions or aspect ratio the same. Then remove the extra margin before slicing the cards to make them equally sized.

To cut the cards you can use a paper trimmer. It takes 4 cuts to slice a sheet of paper with cards into 9 cards. To know where to cut, please use the above-mentioned card measures. There are no cutting marks in the PDF file.

 If you don't have a paper trimmer then you can use a sharp knife and a ruler. Be careful and don't take too many paper sheets in one cut.

It is possible to use colored paper to distinguish the different cards decks of the main game and expansion packs. For instance, you can use white for the main Agile cards, green for Kanban cards, blue for Scrum, etc. This is why the cards are in black and white only (except for the expansion mark), it makes it possible to print them on color paper.

Currently, the cards are only available in PDF downloadable format. There is no printed edition yet.

 If you need multiple physical decks of cards, please contact me to discuss the possibilities.

# Preselecting Cards

The main game consists of 52 cards, the expansion packs vary in number from 26 to 52 cards. In many situations, using cards from the main game and one or more expansion packs would give too many cards to play with.

The solution is to preselect cards and play the game with a subset of the cards.

 Preselecting is a kind of prioritization, it brings focus to the game.

If you already know one or more topics that the team wants to discuss, then you can use those to select cards that are relevant.

 Be sure to select cards that have different views on the topic, to support in-depth discussions.

Alternatively, you can involve one or more team members when preselecting cards. The advantage is that it will give more buy-in from the team as team members were involved early.

 If this is your first time playing the game with a specific team, and there's no topic to focus on, then my suggestion is to use only the 52 cards of the main Agile deck.

Sometimes it happens that, while playing a game, the team doesn't relate to a specific card or considers it to be irrelevant for them. Often they are right, so usually it works best to just ignore that card and take it out of the game.

There are plenty of cards, focus on the ones that help the team to find improvements that make sense to them.

 If you're in doubt on how to preselect cards or what to include or exclude, feel free to contact me!

# Basic Game Playing Format

The most basic way to play a game with the cards is to have team members take turns on the cards and discuss them:

- Team member picks a card and reads it out loud
- The team discusses to assess how well it's done:
  1. Not or inconsistently done
  2. Consistently done, but the value can be increased
  3. Consistently done, valuable practice for the team
- Put the card on stack 1, 2, or 3 and next team member picks next card
- After playing some cards, consider cards in 1&2 for improvement and decide what to do

This suggestion is included in the last but one card of the game. It's an easy way to start with the game and support teams to discuss their current practices and look for improvements.

# Variants on the Basic Game

Variants to play the basic game are:

- Instead of discussing a card, team members vote on a scale from 1-5 how good a practice mentioned on a card is done. The facilitator notes the scores. Discuss the cards with many high or low votes or where there is a big spread in the votes.
- Divide the cards between the team members. Team members take turns, every turn a team member picks only one card from her/his deck of cards that (s)he wants to discuss.
- Prioritize the cards on how well the practice is being done with the whole team. Discuss only the top and bottom 3 cards; well-implemented practices and those that need improvement. When 52 cards are too much, then make a preselection of cards (15 or more) to prioritize.
- Use your imagination to think of another way to play the game ...

# Health Check

At times you want to know how agile you are, and explore if the way that you're using agile practices is still effective. With a health check, you can self-assess how well you are doing. Over time teams can see where and how they have improved and decide where to focus their improvement energy.

 You can do an agile health check using the cards from the Agile Self-assessment Game with a radar chart.

To prepare for a health check, the team decides which agile topics they would like to self-assess. My suggestion is to agree upon 4 to 8 different topics in one assessment.

Preferably those topics are related, for instance, different topics about team working, continuous improvement, or Scrum practices. If you want to have a broader view of how team(s) are performing, then you can pick more distinct topics.

For each topic, select 5 cards from the agile game or from one or more of the expansion packs (Scrum, Kanban, DevOps, Business Agility). If you initially have more cards than 5 cards, then I suggest keeping the most distinct ones for a topic to have a broader scope and stimulate a diverse view on the topic.

Create a radar chart with an ax for each of the topics, using a scale from 1 to 5:

1. not performing
2. weak performance
3. average performance
4. good performance
5. perfect

Stick the 5 cards at the outside of the radar chart at the axes so that everyone can read them. Together the cards define the topics and can be used to guide discussions. Next, write a header for each topic.

## Game: Health Check

Health Check with Radar Charts

Each team member assesses how they think the team is performing for each topic. They do this by placing a dot on the level on the ax for that topic.

 Often it's interesting to explore the differences in scoring, for instance where one or a few persons score differently from the majority. The goal of the discussions is to create a shared understanding and align where needed.

After completing the radar chart, you can decide where you would like to improve as a team. Pick only one or two topics, and agree as a team on the vital few actions that will help you to increase your performance on that topic. Make it specific and actionable.

A health check game can also be done with people from multiple teams. It will help them to discuss how they do things, share experiences, and learn from each other. There is no wrong or right or best way; just good ideas.

If you want to monitor how your team(s) are improving, then health checks can be a very powerful tool. You can collect the scores per topic (min, max, and average) in an Excel or Google sheet and look at the trend over time after doing a couple of assessments.

 The data from health checks should never be used to judge or reward teams. Also, don't try to compare or rank different teams using results from a health check (or any other self-assessment).

Teams will not be honest in their scores if they find out that you are using their data for such purposes, doing that kills the spirit of self-assessment and improvement!

# Investing in Agile

It can be hard for agile teams to decide what they will do to improve their way of working. Often there are multiple problems that they like to solve, and addressing all of them at the same time is not feasible nor effective. As a team, you need to decide where to invest in agile.

This playing suggestion can be used by teams who want to agree on what to improve next. Teams can ask one or more of their stakeholders to join the game so that they can decide together where and how they will invest to improve their agility.

Playing the game starts by shuffling the cards and dividing the cards among the team members.

On turns, each team member picks a card from their hand where (s)he thinks the team needs to work on, plays it by putting it on the table in front of the whole team, and explains why (s)he thinks the team needs to do the practice mentioned on the card.

 Pick the card that you think is most important for the team at this moment, the one which would help the team most given how they are doing at the moment.

After the team members have confirmed that they understand it (it's not necessary that they agree) the next team member plays one card and explains why it's important.

When there are sufficient cards on the table (usually after 2-3 rounds or when you have 15-20 cards on the table) the whole team looks at them and tries to cluster them into groups. Look for cards which are related to the same topic, cards that will probably need similar actions, or involve the same people.

Now each team member gets a fixed amount of coins (between 3-7, depending on the number of cards) which represent the investment that the team can make to improve themselves. All team members put their coins on the cluster or on a specific card of which they think the team should work on. If you don't have any coins, use candy, gummy bears, pins, etc. No peanuts please, you know the saying ;-).

 It's allowed and even recommended to put more coins on the same card or cluster, as that helps the team to focus.

After all team members have decided where they think the team should invest, take a look at the clusters and cards that got the most coins. For those cards, recap the why and write it down together with the card text on a whiteboard or flip-over, or on a laptop using screen sharing with a beamer or flat screen.

Now that it is clear where the team wants to invest, they can discuss what they will do and how to do it. Decide on the actions and note them down.

# Sailboat Retrospective with the Game

Many teams use the sailboat retrospective exercise to reflect on what's holding them back and what is helping them to reach their goal, their island in the sun. The Agile Self-assessment Game can be played by teams using a similar sailboat metaphor.

Teams can play the game in a sailboat retrospective when they want to explore how well they are performing agile practices, or as a sailboat futurespective to set course on their agile journey.

 This playing suggestion is also suitable for teams who are familiar with the sailboat retrospective exercise and would like to do it in a different way.

Draw the sailboat as described in my book Getting Value out of Agile Retrospectives on a large piece of paper (flip chart):

- Destination (an island in the sun) representing the goal that your team wants to reach
- The wind, all the things that help us to go forward
- The anchor, things that slow us down
- Rocks, risks that might happen during the journey toward the island

Put the paper down in middle of the table so that all team members can see it.

The facilitator explains the image and the metaphor to the team. Next, the cards are shuffled and divided among the team members.

At turns, each team member picks a card and places it on the flip chart at the spot where (s)he thinks it belongs. If it's a team strength that they are doing well, something that helps the team, then put it at the wind. If it's something that the team is not doing well, which is hampering the team and slowing them down, then put it on the anchor. Something that might pose a risk in the future can be put on the rocks.

When all cards have been played the team looks at the sheet and discusses the situation that they are in. They can pick one or more cards from the anchor to work on, where they can use strengths on the cards at the wind to address it. Or they can decide to work on one of the risks by selecting a card from the rocks.

 Write down actions that come out of the discussions so that the team knows what has been decided and how to go forward.

# First Things First

When you start with a new product or project, there are many things that teams need to arrange to work together. You can't do everything at the same time, it helps to focus and establish first things first so that teams can take off.

This playing suggestion can be used by new teams who want to agree on what to do first, or existing teams that get a new assignment and have to figure out what is most important.

 Teams can ask their stakeholders to join the game so that they can decide together and get their support and commitment where needed.

Playing the game starts by shuffling the cards. Next, every team member gets 2 cards. Don't show the cards to the other players. The remaining cards are put face down in middle as a stack.

The first team member takes the top card from the stack and reads it. Don't tell other team members what is on the card. Then (s)he can decide to keep it if (s)he thinks this is important. Optionally (s)he can throw one of the two cards already in possession away as it is less important.

If the player thinks that it is less important than the cards that (s)he has already, then she can throw it away by putting it face-up in front of the stack. If she doesn't know for sure or doesn't want to decide yet, then (s)he can keep it for now.

At the end of the round, a player has 2 or 3 cards, depending on if (s)he decided to keep one extra card or not.

The next player can take a card from the top of the stack (face down, so you don't know what is on the card) or take the card that is visible in front of the stack (that the other player threw away). Next (s)he decides to keep it or throw it away by putting it on top of the face-up cards in front of the stack.

A player should never have more than 3 cards in his/her hand. If you go over this, then you have to decide which card to throw away before you end your turn.

**First Things First**

After a couple of rounds, all players decide which 2 cards they want to keep. If they have 3 cards then they need to throw one away. Next, they put their cards visible in front of them and explain to the team why they kept these cards, why they think that they are important.

Next, all cards are assembled together and the whole team looks at them and tries to cluster them into groups. Look for cards which are related to the same topic, cards that will probably need similar actions, or involve the same people.

If there are still too many cards or clusters, then the team can vote which one they want to do first and next, or rank the clusters in order of priority.

Now that it is clear what the team wants to do first, they can discuss what they will do and how to do it. Decide on the actions and note them down.

As a variant, you can introduce an extra round after 2-3 rounds where every player blindly picks a card from their neighbor which is either taken out of the game (impossible to do the thing mentioned on the card) or put at the bottom of the face-down stack (might be possible later). Or they can do an extra round where each player gives one of their cards to their neighbor, which the neighbor can decide to keep or throw away (this is about trust, expecting that your fellow team members will do the right thing with your card).

# Deep Thought

 "Yes," said Deep Thought. "Life, the Universe, and Everything. There is an answer. But, I'll have to think about it."
Douglas Adams, The Hitchhiker's Guide to the Galaxy

For this game assume that you are a team who want to agree on what's needed to get started with agile. Before taking off on your agile journey your team members want time to think to come up with the answer to the ultimate question of agile (and life, the universe, and everything):

What is the single thing that is most needed now to work agile as a team.

Playing the game starts by shuffling the cards. Next, the cards are divided over four stacks of equal size. The stacks are put face down on the table in the middle where all players can access them.

The first player picks one of the four stacks, looks at the cards, and takes two cards which (s)he thinks are most important for the team to work in an agile way. Don't tell other players which cards you took. The player then puts the stack back face down.

Going clockwise, the next player picks a stack and selects two cards. This continues until the last player, who get two turns: (s)he can pick two times two cards. It can be from different stacks or two cards from the same stack.

Now go back anti-clockwise to the previous player who takes two cards from one of the stacks. Continue until you reach the first player, now everyone has four cards.

The four stacks are a kind of gamification; they sim-
ulate that you can actually never oversee or know
everything. There will be things in the other stacks
that you can't access (but other players might pick
that stack).

Now take your time to think about what's really the most important
thing. Every player looks at the cards that they have to decide which
one describes the thing that is most needed now to work agile as a
team.

You can rank your cards from most to least important,
compare pairs to decide which is more important;
whatever works for you.

Please be silent and allow people to think.

When everyone is ready thinking, then the first player shows
their card and explains to the team why they think it's the most
important thing to do. Other players listen to understand, no
discussion is allowed.

When all players have explained their cards, then the cards are
assembled together. The whole team looks at them and together
they think about solutions to reach the statement mentioned on
the card.

Next, discuss what you will do and how to do it. Then decide on
the actions and note them down.

As a variant, you can do a single round where each player takes
three cards from a stack. Next, the players work in pairs of two
where they discuss their cards and then pick only one card from

the six that they have together, being the one they agree is most important for the team to work in an agile way. They may also think about how to do it, and propose that to the team.

 "The Answer to the Great Question... Of Life, the Universe and Everything... Is... Forty-two," said Deep Thought, with infinite majesty and calm.
Douglas Adams, The Hitchhiker's Guide to the Galaxy

# Best Agile Practice Contest

This playing suggestion can be used to discover, reward, and share effective agile practices in one team or between multiple teams in an organization.

To play this variant, you need cards from the main Agile game and if you want from the expansion packs, a dice, blank papers (A4 or letter format), markers and pens to create a mini-poster, and coins to vote.

The first step for playing this variant is to agree on the topic of the agile practice contest so that people will know what kind of practices to look for.

Examples of topics are:

- Best Scrum practice
- Best technical practice
- Most effective approach or exercise to do in agile retrospectives
- Best technique for continuous integration or continuous delivery
- Greatest way to collaborate in teams or with stakeholders
- Most useful Scrum master practices
- Best planning or tracking technique
- ...

The game facilitator will preselect cards that match with the topic of the context. Use cards from the main Agile game and from one or more of the expansion packs (Scrum, Kanban, DevOps, Business Agility, etc).

 As a minimum, there should be twice as many cards as there are players. As a maximum I would go for three times as many, to prevent that players lose too much time going through many cards.

A "best agile practice" is something that the team does. It can come from the current team or from teams that players worked in previously.

 The best practice can also be an idea that someone wants to try out and experiment with in the team.

At the start of the game, all cards are put visibly on the table. On turns, each player throws the dice. The player with the highest score starts by picking one card from the cards that are visible on the table which reminds her/him of a best agile practice, and briefly explains the practice to the other players. Then the player puts the card in front of her/him.

The remaining players will throw the dice, again the one who has the highest score selects a card and explains their best agile practice. This continues until all players have selected a card.

Every player now creates a mini-poster that explains their best agile practice related to the card that they picked. On their poster they can explain how the practice is done, the benefits they got from doing the practice, things they learned, and anything else that will help to convince and sell to the other players that it is the best agile practice.

Next everyone presents their mini-poster and tries to sell their best practice to the other players.

 My suggestion is to time-box the presentations with a stopwatch, for instance, give 1 minute to each player. It should be an elevator pitch, short and focused.

After all players have presented their best practice, the players vote for the greatest agile practice. Every player has three votes (coins, candy, gummy bears, etc), they can give maximum one vote to their own practice. The winner is the one whose practice receives the most votes.

When you play this game with multiple teams, then teams can share their best agile practice after playing the game within their team. The game can stop there as a practice sharing between teams, or you can add another voting round to come to a top 3 or top 5 of best agile practices for the whole organization.

# Worst Agile Practice Contest

An alternative to the best agile practice contest described in the previous section is to do a "worst agile practice contest" where people will share their biggest failures.

 You can preselect cards to focus the topic of the contest or you can use all 52 cards from the main Agile deck to have a broad contest were any agile practice where the team failed can be brought up.

The aim of a worst agile practice contest is to celebrate failure and to learn from it. The mini-poster can be used to explain the failure, visualize the impact, and where possible dive into the root causes.

 Players have to feel psychologically safe to bring up worst practices. When you are unsure if this safety exists, then I suggest using another playing suggestion from this book.

After presenting the failures, the players vote to select one problem that they would like to work on and prevent that it will happen again in the future.

# Sketching your Agile Journey

Agile is not a destination, it's a journey of questioning, exploring, and sharing ideas, in order to uncover better ways of developing software. An excellent way to start this journey is by sketching an initial backlog for it.

 This playing suggestion combines discussion with visualization which is a very effective form of communication in an agile team.

When agile is relatively new for your organization then I suggest playing this game with the 52 cards from the basic game. Together these cards cover all agile values and principles; they will provide you with sufficient and valuable ideas to embark on your agile journey.

 If there is a specific agile practice area where you want to focus your improvement then you can preselect cards from the main Agile deck and expansion packs that cover that area.

Aim to have 30 to 50 cards so that the team can oversee them and decide which ones to pull into their journey.

Playing the game starts by putting the (preselected) cards face-up on the table. The whole team looks at the cards and discusses what are the most valuable topics which need to be improved for the coming time. From the available cards, they select the cards with topics that they want to work on as a team.

 It's better to focus on what's most important. My suggestion is to pick maximum 10 cards.

The cards which are not selected are taken out of the game and can be put aside on a stack.

After selecting the cards, the team ranks them in order of priority of what to do first and what to do next. Together they decide what is most important now and what can be done later but is still needed to get started.

Now the team creates an initial backlog of improvement items which are related to the selected cards, beginning with the most valuable card. This is done by sticking the cards on a flip-over sheet (in order of priority).

Next to each card, the team shares ideas about how to improve the related topic by sketching some initial wishes or even concrete actionable tasks (for instance using sticky notes).

When the last card has been explored, the team members reflect on the backlog in order to decide if they are all on the same page regarding the outcome.

 It's important to check if everybody is committed starting the agile journey they just explored and visualized.

During the game or after finishing the backlog, the team might consider changing the order of the backlog items if they see a need for that.

And of course, they can (and probably will) change priorities once they are executing the backlog and traveling their agile journey, based on how they are doing.

 As a facilitator, you have to stay alert whether the team is making progress and doesn't become silent or gets stuck in long discussions. Coach the team to prevent them from deviating too far from the process and losing their focus.

When playing with multiple teams, the teams can present their agile journey backlog to other teams and explain the actions that they will take and their expectations of the outcomes.

The playing suggestion Sketching your Agile Journey was created by Berry Kersten. Berry and I first played it at the Amsterdam Agile Showcase 2018.

# Learning by Sharing Challenges

The sharing challenges playing format enables cross-organizational learning, for instance between professionals from different departments, multiple teams from a project or product, managers that are spread throughout the organization, or any combination of this.

This game format makes it possible to explore the main challenges that professionals have and would like would like to work on and to identify existing solutions to challenges that they previously faced and solved.

To use this game playing suggestion, put all the cards face-up on the table. Next, ask the players to place cards on a flipover sheet with two big circles: one for the challenges that they are currently facing and one for challenges that they managed to solve.

**Sharing Challenges**

Every player can pick a card and put it in the circle where it fits for them, depending on if it's something that they are dealing with right now or something they solved.

What will happen next is that players will want to move cards to the overlapping area, e.g. when they are facing a problem that a previous player put a card for in "challenges we solved" or when they solved a challenge that another player is facing and put in "challenges we have".

 It is only allowed to move cards from one of the circles to the overlapping area, not swap between the circles (that would probably trigger discussions which don't have any value in them).

The overlapping area is where the interesting stuff is. It's the challenges players are facing where there are solutions at the table from other players. This is where players can share and learn from each other!

There can also be major challenge(s) in the "challenges we have" circle where players can team up and work together to solve them on an organizational level. That would be a more effective and efficient approach to increase the agility of the whole organization over each team working in isolation on their own challenges.

As there are many cards (197 in all decks together) you might want to do some preselection and play the game with a smaller set. Then you can have all cards visible from the start to get discussions going early.

 Possible ways to preselect are by topic/focus setting (for instance only cards related to team working, to culture, or to a specific practice area like continuous delivery, how we do Scrum, etc.) or by only inserting one card where there are overlapping cards (one card on retrospectives, one on handling impediments, etc).

This is not a game in the strict sense that there are winners or losers; actually, everyone wins if they share and collaborate. It's a gamification where principles and practices of gaming are used in a non-game context, in this case a business context. Which makes it a fun and valuable thing to spend some time on :-).

# Sailboat Futurespective

Teams can play the Agile Self-assessment Game as a sailboat futurespective to find ways toward their goals before they take off. Futurespectives help teams to reach their goals, by putting themselves in the future and exploring how they got there they can discuss and decide on different strategies, opportunities, risks, and approaches.

The facilitator draws the sailboat on a large piece of paper (flip chart) and explains the metaphor that will be used:

- Destination (an island in the sun) representing the goal that the players want to reach
- The wind, all the things that help us to go forward
- The anchor, things that slow us down
- Rocks, risks that might happen during the journey toward the island

Put the paper in the middle of the table so that all players see it. Shuffle the cards and divide them among the players.

The facilitator asks the players to put themselves in the future and imagine that they are an awesome team where people worked together to deliver great products. Each player looks at the cards that they have to imagine what they did to become such a great team.

At turns, each player picks one card from their hand and places it on the chart.

 If it's something your imaginary team does well, something that helps them, then put it at the wind. If it's something not going well, hampering the team and slowing them down, then put it on the anchor. Something that has posed a risk can be put on the rocks.

After a first round, the players explain their card and discuss them. They share experiences, what has worked for them and what didn't work, and why.

Then they do a next round, until all cards have been played or a predefined time limit is reached.

When all cards are played, the team comes back from the future. Next, the players discuss what they can do to become an awesome team, and how to deal with the challenges on their journey. They agree on what they will do today to start their journey to become a great team, and note down the actions that they will take.

# Angel's Advocate

The Angel's Advocate is a technique to stimulate creative and positive thinking and come up with new ideas.

You use this technique by asking people to come up with an idea. Players then react by saying what they like about the idea, how to enhance it and build on it, what benefits they see, and how it can create value.

This motivates the submitter of the idea, and encourages the group to come up with more positive ideas. The group members become engaged and will stimulate each other to think creatively.

 Some would call this "thinking outside the box", but actually there are no boxes :-).

All ideas are collected during the session, e.g. on a flip chart. At the end, the group can pick the ones which are most promising, and decide when and how to implement them.

 Critical remarks are not allowed during the session!

You can play the Agile Self-assessment Game using the Angel's Advocate suggestion to explore your agile journey up to now and continue your travels. The cards from this game can be used to come up with positive ideas where the team works together to improve them.

For example, assuming that someone plays the following card from the game:

> The team does not rely on management to set and meet its goals

The team members can build on this by saying:

> We know what our customers really need

> Yes, and we can ask them what they would like to have next

> And we can also ask them how they would use it and what value it would bring them

> Actually, we have data that tells us which functions our customers are using

> And we know how to develop and test new functions

> Wow, together we can really deliver value if we use all of the things we already have and know as a team and work together!

You may say that the Angels Advocate looks like a brainstorm session, but there is a big difference. In a brainstorm, members of the group do not state any opinions about the ideas, neither negative nor positive.

 The role of the Angel's Advocates is to explicitly react positively to ideas, thus rewarding the submitter for her/his contribution.

You might also know the Devil's Advocate. Playing this role stimulates a discussion in which we challenge ideas in order to improve them.

 There can be a place and time to be critical and be the Devil's Advocate, but we need more positive thinking, and more Angel's Advocates.

This technique and related positive psychology-based methods like Appreciative Inquiry and Solution Focused (in Dutch: Oplossingsgericht Werken) can help you to come up with great ideas and deliver creative value.

# Two Truths and a Lie

This playing format for the Agile Self-assessment Game is based on the classic two truths and a lie icebreaker. It usually works best within new teams for people to get to know each other.

 In some cases it can also be played in existing teams to learn what people believe in and consider to be important or not important in their daily work.

In this playing format, people tell two truths and one lie. The objective of the game is to discover the lie and get to learn each other and hear about things people believe in or not believe in.

The setup for this game is to sit in a circle. You can use chairs or people can sit on the ground if that feels comfortable enough for them. It helps to have a table nearby and for instance use a tray where you put the cards on. Alternatively, you can sit around a table, but then you will miss some of the none verbal communication that's hidden away behind the table.

The facilitator explains how the game will be played and that the aim is to learn about each other.

 If the players don't know each other yet, they can briefly introduce themselves.

Playing the game starts by shuffling the cards. Next, the cards are divided over four stacks of equal size. The stacks are put face down on the table or tray where all players can access them.

The first player picks one of the four stacks, looks at the cards, and takes two cards which (s)he thinks are agile principles or practices that (s)he strongly believes in and does her/himself; things that are important for the whole team to know. Don't show the cards. Then the next player picks a stack and selects two cards.

After all of the players have picked two cards with things they believe in and do in their daily work, they do another round but now each player picks one card that triggers them about something that they don't believe in, a thing they generally don't do or would prefer not to do.

After all players have selected the cards and took time to prepare their statements, go around the circle where each player uses their cards to tell two truths and one lie.

Now it's up to the players to guess the false ones, the lies. You can have a voting, or everybody can say for each person which statement they think is the lie.

 Remember, it's not a competition about who finds the most lies. It can be fun to discover a lie, or to completely miss a lie and really learn something about somebody.

Let's give an example. After going through the cards and picking two cards I believe in and one that I have serious doubts about, I might say:

It's important to keep a constant pace in our team to prevent getting overloaded

I believe that we have to involve everyone when we plan our sprint

Retrospectives are the main driver to reflect, learn, and improve

People who know me, know that the last statement is something that I really believe and do, so that's an easy one. But what about the first and second? Which one is true and which one is a lie?

Let me help you out. For me, the second statement is a lie. I don't believe that it's feasible nor effective to always involve everyone in every planning sessions. Sure, it's good to have different views and giving people a say increase their involvement and hence gets them more committed to the result. But involving everyone in everything simply doesn't work; that's my belief.

Now you learned something about me that you didn't know before! You might agree or disagree. Have a strong opinion yourself. That's ok, but remember that the goal of this game is to get to learn each other, not to judge.

 If you find out during the game that one of the lies (or a truth) is important and would need an alignment for the whole team, then you can decide to discuss it. Don't do this however before all players have presented their statements and all lies have been guessed.

Two truths and a lie is a fun game, doing it with the Agile Self-assessment Cards can help teams to find out how people truly feel about the agile mindset, principles, and practices.

 There is no right or wrong, working together in a team is about people who have their own beliefs, and that's ok.

# More Ideas for Playing the Game

New ideas and playing formats for the Agile Self-assessment Game come to existence in varies way. Sometimes I come up with something new when I'm preparing a workshop for a client. Or I get an idea for playing with the cards when giving a public workshop or attending an open space or unconference.

This section contains ideas and thoughts that haven't been worked out into a full playing suggestion yet. Use them as inspiration, feel free to pick them up and experiment.

 If you try them out, it would be great if you share your experiences with me and with the readers of this book. Please reach out to me!

### Consent Decision Making from Sociocracy

In 2017 I attended a workshop on Sociocracy 3.0 by James Priest. One of the things that struck me was consent decision making as an alternative for consensus or democratic decisions.

 I've been using consent to help people make decisions and have found it to be very effective. It's quick, you can get people really involved, and it inspires people to take action.

I'm thinking about creating a playing suggestion where people would pick cards that they would like to experiment with, and then use consent to decide as a team to do it.

 My suggestion is to use "good enough for now, safe enough to try" from sociocracy 3.0 as a guiding idea to try out new things, and agree on a single thing that the team would do next.

### 1-2-4-all from Liberating Structures

The 1-2-4-all structure proposes a format where ideas that people come up with are discussed in pairs, then foursomes, and finally as a whole group.

 At various open spaces I experienced how a 1-2-4-all exercise from Liberating Structures helps to engage people, generate new ideas, and align their thinking to come to something actionable that has buy-in.

The idea would be to offer cards from the Agile Self-assessment Game and have people pick one card that they would like to work with. Next, do the 1-2-4-all and see what comes out at the end.

### Exploring Strengths

What if we could use the cards to identify team or individual strengths? Reward people for great things that they do? Recognize behavior that helps the team and create conditions for it to happen more?

 I'm a big fan of positive approaches like Appreciative Inquiry, Angel's Advocate, and Solution Focused. We don't need failure to learn, we can also get better by exploring things that go well.

This playing format could be something similar to the retrospective exercise Exploring Strengths with Core Qualities where team members are asked to identify core qualities or strengths that they have recognized in one or more of their team members.

During the game, people could bring up a major challenge and then explore how it can be solved using the strengths that they identified.

# Experience Stories

This chapter provides experience stories from myself and from others who played the game.

Their purpose is to inspire you and share how the game is being played, and learn what the game might do for you and your teams.

# Playing the Agile Self-assessment Game at XP Days 2016

 I (Ben Linders) played the Agile Self-Assessment game at XP Days Benelux 2016 with three teams. This was the first public appearance with the game.

I started by explaining the game, and then the teams took off playing it. They had multiple exercises from which they could choose, but all teams decided to play the "new team" exercise which is a kind of pro-spective or futurespective.

The aim of the new team exercise is to help teams to decide on the vital few things that they need to set up before or during their first iteration to get started:

> You are a new team, preparing for a first iteration. Things need to be arranged and you have to decide how to work together, but there's just too much that needs to be done. You need to agree on what to do now to quickly become a productive agile team capable to deliver.

It was great to see the teams playing the game. They had lively discussions about the cards, sometimes to their surprise as team members expected many things to be obvious. Well, it often isn't.

To give an example: One team discussed the card which mentioned: "There is an automated build and regression test". Some of the team members, particularly the ones who are developers, argued that this is something that for sure needs to be done in the first iteration. Other team members doubted if it is really that important, and if you can actually do this in a couple of weeks. "Sure, no problem" was the answer they got. In the end, some teams decided that they would do it in the first iteration, some not.

Of course, there is no right answer, it depends a lot on the context that the team is in. Some teams actually went deeper and discussed when you would need it and when you can postpone it. In the evaluation at the end of the game, several people mentioned how valuable these discussions have been. Isn't that a cool thing to hear!

**Debriefing at XP Days, image by Ahmad Atwi**

Some other feedback I got was that the game helps teams to brainstorm about their way of working. The cards trigger fruitful discussions which provide valuable insights.

Team members also get to learn each other in the game, and they find out how their colleagues feel about certain practices. One attendee said that it was nice to experience that prioritizing is not always easy, he gained an understanding of what their product owner feels when the team wants to know what to do first.

 I asked the teams to also note down improvement suggestions for the game, which they did. So it wasn't only the attendees who learned things in my session, I also learned stuff. This is one of the reasons why I like the XP Days Benelux conference so much, you ask for feedback, and you get it!

# Help Scrum and Agile Teams Improve

 Andreas Schliep, Executive Partner at DasScrumTeam AG, shared his experiences playing this game in Agile Self-Assessment by Ben Linders. Here's what he wrote on LinkedIn Pulse, extended with some more details from our discussion on his learnings.

Scrum and Agile teams want to become better. In the beginning, improvement is actually easy to identify and hard to accomplish. The first steps of changing an existing team setup to a suitable frame for agile work are probably well known. Yes, it is hard. Yes, it takes time. And after a while, most teams actually have a proper Product Owner, get decent management support, can organize their work themselves.

Things get harder, once teams have reached a certain basic level. Instead of raising the same fuzzy wishes towards the organization, teams could try a different approach. This is where the Agile Self-Assessment Game by Ben Linders comes into play.

The gameplay may vary, but mostly the discussion revolves around three major points:

- What agile practices are important for our team?
- How good are we at fulfilling them?
- How can we improve?

I played this game with a software development team recently. We used a variation of the gameplay that came out as a result of Ben's Open Space session about the game at the retrospective facilitators gathering.

After I distributed the cards evenly, the team members selected one very important card from their hand. Then we ranked these cards using a method created by members of a previous Scrum Master in-service training, Backlog Ranking.

 As it turned out, the method was extremely useful for discussing practices and improvement opportunities.

Afterward, the team members evaluated their fulfillment of these points. We set up a score from 0% to 100%, and the team shifted the cards on the table according to that score.

We did not discuss everything in detail but gained some valuable insights during this exercise. Based on these insights the team decided to take action.

For instance, they agreed to trade estimation accuracy for speed in order to allow for longer-term delivery forecasts and to invest in mutual learning and code base improvements.

I really recommend the Self Assessment Game for Scrum Masters or Agile Teams as a way to facilitate and focus the discussion about possible improvements. In a next step, the team can figure out how to improve in the identified areas on their own, or where they could use the assistance of an agile or technical coach.

# Ideas for playing the Agile Self-assessment Game

 I (Ben Linders) played the Agile Self-assessment game with two teams in a session at the Retrospectives Facilitators Gathering 2017 and discussed the game with several attendees. Below are the ideas that came up for playing the game and for improving it.

A first suggestion that came up was to use Diana Larsen's circles and soup as a playground for the game. Players can put a card in one of the circles "team controls", "team influences", or "soup", depending on how they feel that a team can deal or cannot deal with the practice mentioned on the card.

A dimension that builds on top of that is using a matrix of circles and soup and self-assessment of how well practices are working out.

 One team played this format where attendees self-assessed a team that they are working with by selecting practice cards and placing them in this matrix. This triggered several discussion, like why they felt that improving a practice was within or outside the control of the team, what could be done to gain influence or control, and what could be done to improve the practice.

Another suggestion that came up (actually in both teams) was to rank cards based on the expected value that they can bring to a team. Where estimating the value of a practice can be hard, teams often find it easier to rank practices on value. Ranking reveals the most valuable practices that teams can work on to improve their agility and deliver more value.

One team suggested the game to be played in parallel by one team consisting of executives and another consisting of practitioners, and then combine the results. Seeing where they agree and where there are different insights can lead to useful discussions between them.

Another idea is to do a kind of poker game, where players can keep cards or exchange them with cards on the stack or cards that have been played by other players. It would bring a competitive element into playing the game, which might foster valuable discussions.

Teams can also arrange the practice cards on a matrix with the two dimensions "importance" and "fulfillment", and then select cards from the ones with high importance and low fulfillment to work on.

In some situations, it might be more effective to reduce options and play with fewer cards. Suggestions that came up are to pick a central idea and select cards that support that idea, focus on a specific topic and select cards related to that, or to have the Scrum master or game facilitator pre-select cards based on what the team would need to work on as part of the game preparation.

 In Preselecting Cards I provide ideas on how to select cards from the main Agile deck and expansion packs to create focus and increase effectiveness.

The idea popped up to bring Appreciative Inquire into the game. Players would raise cards with practices which are going well in the team and then think about how to improve even further or use those practices to solve a problem that the team is dealing with.

Next to discovering new ideas to play the game I also looked for ways to improve the game. This is what came up during the week.

One improvement suggestion is to number the cards. That will make it easier to explore similarities and differences when the game is played with multiple teams.

Another improvement is to create double-sided cards, where additional information can be put on the back side of the card.

Powerful questions can also be used to further improve or extend the game. Although the format of questions differs from the statement level used in the game, they can still be used to come up with additional statements or refine the existing ones.

Currently, there are cards with statements that focus on outcomes while other cards mention practices. There's value in both of them, it can be interesting to classify the cards and see what is covered and where there are gaps.

 I want to thank the attendees from the Retrospectives Facilitators Gathering 2017 for playing the game and coming up with great ideas to improve it!

# Playing the Agile Self-assessment Game in Retrospectives

 Marijke Vandermaesen played the game with her team in their agile retrospective. She thinks that "the self-assessment game is a good format for a retrospective". Here are her experiences from playing this game.

A few sprints ago, I (Marijke) facilitated the retrospective of our Scrum team using the Agile Self-assessment Game as the format to guide the retrospective. For preparation, I printed all the 52 cards on paper, cut them into separate cards, set up an online voting system and made a poster with the three columns (not done, done but can be improved, well done).

During the retrospective, each member of the team (we have a quite large team of 8 developers, 3 customer proxies, tech lead, agile coach and team manager) picked one card randomly. I placed some numbers on the back of the cards so I could easily keep track of which cards were done and voted. They read the card out loud for the group and each member used the voting system to give a score on a five-point scale.

After the voting, the members that gave votes that were different from the mean votes, explained themselves and we discussed the card. Each card was then placed on the poster in one of the columns.

After a while, we evaluated the cards in the columns to define smart actions. So far so good. Unfortunately, in the sprint before, we had some escalations due to frustrations and lack of trust between the different teams on our project. This resulted in a downward spiral during the retrospective and some team members lost their appetite for retrospectives because they felt that the core issues in the team were not being discussed and handled. At the end, we only could define one smart action from the cards and had to abandon the rest to define a second smart action to clear the frustrations.

 My (Marijke's) conclusion: the self-assessment game is a good format for a retrospective when being prepared. It can be used in teams that recently started to check which practices to pick up in next sprints, or with experienced teams that already are well adapted to each other to search for new improvements for their teamworking.

You can use the game in several sprints after each other to find issues for all the cards (you cannot do them in one session unless you have a full day retrospective).

However, if your team is experiencing some structural problems or frustrations, clear them out first before using this game.

Marijke Vandermaesen is Functional Analyst /customer proxy at Cegeka.

# Self-assessing How Agile You Are

 In an open space session about Agile Self-Assessments organized by the nlScrum meetup we discussed why self-assessments matter and how teams can self-assess their agility to become better in what they do.

There are many checklists and tools for agile self-assessments. Some of them focus on "hard" things like agile practices, meetings, and roles, while others cover the "soft" aspects like an agile mindset and values, culture, and the conditions for agile adoption in organizations to be successful.

In the meetup we discussed self-assessing team's agility. One conclusion was that most attendants had a strong preference for assessing based on agile values and mindset to explore if and how their teams are becoming agile. This way of assessing distincts teams where professionals have really internalized what agile is and know why they should do it and how it helps them to deliver value to their customers and stakeholder from teams that are only doing agile or Scrum because they have been told to do so by their managers or organization.

 There are many cards in the Agile Self-assessment Game that go back to the agile values and principles. You can use those cards to self-assess the agile mindset.

Assessing values and mindset involves asking why certain agile practices and rituals are done. It empowers the agile team by developing a shared understanding of the weaknesses and strengths of their way of working and to decide which steps they will take to become better.

Effective agile teams understand the agile culture, mindset, and values. That makes it possible for them to improve their development processes in an agile way. They can use the golden rules for agile process improvement to improve by continuously doing small but valuable improvement actions.

 As the name suggests, agile self-assessments are intended to be tools for agile teams. The result of an assessment helps a team to know how they are doing to improve themselves. Therefore the results of an assessment are intended to be used by the team alone. They should not be used by managers to evaluate the team's performance or to compare and rate teams.

At the meetup the question came up if you can expect that a team can assess itself? It depends, as usual :-). Teams who have just started with agile can find it difficult to take some distance and explore how they are doing. They also might not have enough understanding of the why and how of agile to really assess how they are doing. In such cases, an (external) facilitator can coach teams to do their first assessments.

 An agile coach can help a team to develop assessment skills, enabling them to do their own assessments in the future. Soft skills matter in IT and agile coaches can help people to learn and improve those skills. Which is also an effective way to help a team to become agile in an agile way.

# Your Experience Story

If you have played the Agile Self-assessment Game and would like to share your experiences with me, that would be great!

Feel free to reach out to me and tell your story. Let me know how you played the game, how it went, what you learned, and which benefits it has brought you.

Your story can be published as a guest blog on my website. It might also get included in a next edition of this book.

Please contact me by email: benlinders@gmail.com.

# Frequently Asked Questions

This chapter aims to answer any questions that you have about the Agile Self-assessment Game. If your question isn't answered in here, please contact me.

**As an internal Scrum master or internal agile coach, can I play the game with my team(s)?**

Absolutely! Go ahead and download the game and any expansion packs (Scrum, DevOps, Kanban, Business, Agility, etc). that you need, get inspired by the playing suggestions, and start playing it.

**If I'm being paid as a Scrum master or to coach a team, can I use the game in a retrospective?**

The license states that commercial usage is not allowed. However, the game is there to be played, not to collect dust.

You can use it in retrospectives, or on other occasions with teams, as long as you mention my name as the creator of the game and my website as the source where the game can be downloaded.

This also applies when you are an external consultant working with a client (actually the game is bought by consultants all over the world who play it with teams at client's sites). Please do make clear to teams that you work with that the game was developed by Ben Linders, not you.

**Can I share the game with my colleagues or with other professionals like coaches or Scrum masters?**

When you buy the game and expansion packs, you get a personal license to play it. You are not allowed to distribute, share, or transfer the game in any way.

Feel free of course to tell them about the game and give them the URL of the game landing page benlinders.com/game or of the webshop benlinders.com/shop so that they can download their own personal copy of the game and expansion packs to play it.

**What if I'm running a workshop for one or multiple teams, can I use it?**

This is not allowed, as that would be a similar service that I offer commercially through my workshops. The license mentioned in the webshop and on the game, which you also received when you bought the game, states this very clearly.

Then again I don't want to be overly protective which would prevent the game from being used and delivering its value. If you plan to use it in an in-house workshop, please contact me to discuss this. We should be able to formulate a practical license for this, where attribution and recognition for me matter more than money.

Note that if you are interested in offering training which includes one of my games or books, then I do expect you to come to one of my workshops to learn about the game before teaching others.

**Can you do an on-site workshop to teach us how to use the game?**

Of course! I do plenty of those, either as a one-time event or within a consultancy agreement with companies. Often playing games is part of a series of workshops, or I'm asked to do another workshop after some time. I'm flexible, contact me to discuss your needs!

I regularly fly in to do on-site workshops all around the world, one-time gigs are perfectly ok for me.

**Can you come to us to do assessments within our company?**

I can come over to facilitate self-assessments within your company, helping teams to find out how well they are doing and explore how they can further improve themselves. That would be paid work of course, as it increases the value of your teams and your company.

Note that I would not be assessing your teams or the company with the game, I'm supporting and teaching how you can do it yourselves. After I leave, you will be able to do self-assessments with the game.

If you want an assessment, that's a different service which I do provide, for instance with CMMI assessments and audits.

Where there are companies that "abuse" self-assessment as marketing leads for getting consultancy work, I don't do that. I'm not offering "free" assessments to get in and sell consultancy hours.

I don't do full-time consultancy or longer term part-time consultancy. I work with many customers in parallel, delivering just-in-time training, advice, and coaching.

**If I'm being paid by a client should I just not use the material at all?**

You are allowed to use my games, books, and any other products from me under the conditions described above. Just as I want teams to play the game, I'd like consultants and coaches to support playing it. The game is there to be played, not to be hidden away or protected!

So I allow coaches and consultants to play it with teams that they work with. And I love to hear from them how that works out.

Doing training or workshops that includes one or more games is strictly prohibited. If you see a market for a workshop with one of my games or books in the area where you live or work, please let me know. Then I'd like to partner with you to offer public and/or in-house workshops.

**Why do you make the game available for other consultants and coaches?**

Part of my business is giving workshops (in-house and public) and doing on-site advisory and coaching work, where the games and exercises that I use significantly drive the value that I deliver.

I'm trying to find a balance between providing tools that teams and coaches can use in their daily work and services like workshops, training, and advice, to organizations for sustainable change. Both aim to increase agility and result in better software products and services, which is my contribution to making this world a little bit better. Both have value, that's why started selling the game through my webshop.

Also scaling plays a role here. I can't possibly train all organizations and teams who want to play the game. But I can provide the game through my webshop and (remotely) support facilitators all around the world when playing it :-).

It's a pleasure for me to support consultants and coaches if they want to play the game, so feel free to reach out to me.

**In my company, there are several facilitators that want to play the game. Do they all have to buy their personal copy of the game?**

When someone buys a game or expansion pack, they get a personal license to play it. So one solution is that every facilitator buys his/her own game to be allowed to play it. But with many facilitators inside a company, that can be a hassle.

There's a better deal, which is the Agile Self-assessment Game - Corporate Edition.

The corporate edition provides ten licenses for facilitators to play the game within the company. It contains the basic game and all expansion packs, and comes with playing instructions and experience stories, one hour of training, and free lifetime support. You get all of this in one buy, for a reduced price :-)

Instead of a personal license, the corporate edition grants the company a license to have the game played within the company.

**I work with a consultancy agency and I would like the consultants that I hire to play the game with the teams in my company. Is that possible?**

Of course. But then you will have to acquire the Corporate Edition of the game, not have the consultancy agency buying it.

When the Agile Self-assessment Game - Corporate Edition is bought, the corporate license goes to the company that employs the buyer. So the buyer has to be employed by and working for the company where the game is supposed to be played, which is your company.

**What happens if the consultancy agency or a consultant buys the Corporate Edition?**

If the consultancy agency or a consultant buys the corporate edition, then the license allows them to play the game with a maximum of ten facilitators within their own consulting company. The license does not allow them to have their consultants playing the game with their clients!

If a consulting agency wants one of their consultants to play the game with the client's team(s) then that consultant should personally buy the game. Buying the game or an expansion pack gives a personal license to play it by the consultant, where the Corporate Edition comes with a company license.

**I have the Corporate Edition. One of the persons that facilitated playing the game has left. Is it allowed to let another facilitator step in and play the game?**

Yes! The license to play belongs to the company, so the company can transfer it to another employee who will play it within the company.

**I played the game in the company that I worked using the Corporate Edition, but now I left the company and got a new job. Can I play the game in the new company?**

The license that you used to play the game belonged to the company where you used to work. It doesn't allow you to play it in your new company.

I would suggest to either buy the game yourself, which will give you a personal license, or have your new company buy the Corporate Edition and use one of the licenses that comes with it to play the game.

**I'm a consultant and I work with multiple clients. Can I play the game within each of the companies that I work with?**

Yes, you can, provided that you bought the game personally and attribute it to me when playing it (see "If I'm being paid as a Scrum master or to consult or coach a team, can I use the game"). You don't need to buy multiple copies of the game (per client).

Be aware that you are not allowed to use it in training or workshops. Also, it's not allowed to have the game facilitated by an employee from one of your clients or by a colleague since you only have a personal, non-transferable license for playing the game.

**What if I bought the wrong edition of the game?**

That's easy, just contact me. Let me know what happened and what you need, and we'll sort it out.

I'll refund and will adjust the order to make sure that you get what you need, and only pay for that.

**Why do I have to pay for downloading the game?**

Initially, I offered the game for free, but due to the great feedback that I received from those who played it, I decided to ask a small price for downloading it. Apparently, the game brings value, so it makes sense that I ask people to pay for it.

The prices I ask are very reasonable: you can download the game with expansion packs for the price of a good cup of coffee and a tasty muffin; it costs much less than an hour of consultancy (even from a cheap consultant).

The revenue that I receive also warrants the time that I frequently invest in updating the games and adding playing suggestions.

**Is there any guarantee or support for the game?**

I can't give any guarantee, but everything that people/companies buy from me comes with Free Lifetime Support. This is valid for any workshop, training, coaching, or advice that I provide, and also for my games and books.

If you're not happy with any product, anytime, let me know. I refund. When you're happy, or very happy, let me know too :-). Send me an email. Write a guest blog to share your experiences. Let the world know in social media (tag me or use the tag #AssessAgility!). Shout it out!

**Can I get a physical deck of cards?**

The easiest (and currently only) way to have physical cards is to download the game and expansion packs, print them, and slice the pages into individual cards.

Distributing the game in digital format using PDF is the fastest, easiest, and most sustainable solution that I can think of.

This is an agile game, which I develop using Lean Startup and Agile principles and practices. The cards are being updated frequently based on feedback received, more cards are added, and sometimes cards are removed. The digital format allows me to do this and release frequently.

I'm exploring POD solutions like the Game Crafter, MPC, Printer Studio, and ArtsCow, for on-demand production and shipping. They can be used to deliver single decks but at a high price.

If you want to have multiple physical decks for your company, contact me. Pre-order the Agile Self-assessment Cards - Physical Deck to let me know that you are interested. Together we can find a solution.

**How do I make my own deck of cards?**

Start by downloading the game and printing the PDF files. Depending on your expected usage, you can print on normal copier paper (80 g/m2) or heavier paper, or on photo paper.

You might laminate the cards if you intend to use them frequently.

I sometimes use colored paper to distinguish the different cards decks. White for the main game, green for Kanban cards, blue for Scrum, etc. This is why the cards are in black and white only, it makes it possible to print them on color paper.

When you play the game, ask people not to write on the cards if you want to reuse them.

### Do you have an app for the Agile Self-assessment Game?

Not yet. Suggestions on how to do this in a practical way are welcome!

Note that I would highly favor a way to self-develop, release, and support the game as a one-man BusDevOps team. Please don't send me offers to develop an app for me or to outsource app development.

# Assessment Tools and Checklists

Agile is a journey where you learn and improve continuously. Agile Self-assessments help teams to see where they are to decide on the next steps to increase their agility.

If you want to become more Agile and Lean, my recommendation is to frequently ask yourself the following 3 questions:

- How Agile and Lean are you already?
- Where do you want to become more Agile and Lean? And why?
- What can you do to make the next step?

Agile Self-assessments help you to ask these questions and travel your agile journey.

There are many different self-assessment methods, tools, and checklists, that teams and organizations can use to find out how well they are doing agile and what they can improve to become self-organized. For an up-to-date list, please visit Agile Self-assessments.

Note that not all of these tools are true "self-assessing" and some are used as a marketing tool to acquire business. Which is not how I use self-assessments; I teach teams, coaches, and managers how they can use self-assessment as an "agile map" for their journey of continuous improvement.

# Tools and Checklists for Agile Self-assessments

The following tools and checklists are known to me (70++). They can help you to do a kind of startup/health check or readiness/maturity assessment to determine how agile or lean you are:

- My Agile Self-Assessment Game
- The Unofficial Scrum Checklist from Henrik Kniberg
- 42 point test: How Agile are You by Kelly Waters
- Questions for Transitioning to Agile from Johanna Rothman
- Agile Adoption Framework by Ahmed Sidky
- Team Barometer by Jimmy Janlén
- Scrum Checklist by Boris Gloger
- Corporate Agile 10-point checklist by Elena Yatzeck
- Joe's Unofficial Scrum Checklist by Joe Little
- Lean-Agile Roadmap by NetObjectives
- ScrumButt Test aka the Nokia Test by Jeff Sutherland
- How to Measure Team Agility by Len Lagestee
- Scrum Assessment Series by David Hawks
- Agile Maturity Self Assessment by Robbie Mac Iver
- Enterprise Agility Maturity Matrix by Eliassen Group
- Enterprise Agile Practice Assessment Tool (paid services) by DrAgile
- Comparative Agility by Mike Cohn and Kenny Rubin
- Open Assessments from scrum.org
- Readiness & Fit Analysis from the Software Engineering Institute by Suzanne Miller
- Agile Journey Index by Bill Krebs
- Seven Questions to Ask to Determine if Your Organization is Agile Ready from PMI Austin
- An Organizational Transformation Checklist by Michael Sahota

- Agile Maturity Matrix in JIRA by Atlassian
- Assessing your Client's Agility by Marcel Britsch
- Borland Agile Assessment
- Agile Self Assessment by Cape Project Management
- Agile Maturity Model (AMM) by Chetankumar Patel and Muthu Ramachandran
- Test your Organisation's Agile Credentials by Storm-Consulting
- Depth of Kanban by Christophe Achouiantz
- Agile Essentials (card game) by Ivar Jacobson International
- IBM DevOps Practices Self Assessment
- Agile team evaluation by Eric Gunnerson
- Ready for Agile Part 1 and Part 2 by Salah Elleithy (based on research by Ahmed Sidky)
- Squad Health Check model from Spotify / Henrik Kniberg
- Assessing the level of Agility by Yuval Yeret
- Assess your Agility by James Shore
- Test Maturity card game by Joep Schuurkes and Huib Schoots
- AgilityHealth Radar (paid service)
- Rojooms How Deep is your Agile? by Shirly Ronen-Harel
- Agile 3R Model of Maturity Assessment by Phani Thimma-puram
- Cargo Cult Agile Checklist by Age of Product
- Success Factors for Self-Assessment of Teams by Angelika Drach, Christoph Mathis & Jens Coldewey
- Your Path through Agile Fluency by Diana Larsen and James Shore & Finding Agile That's Fit-for-Purpose by Diana Larsen
- The InfoQ Minibook Scrum Hard Facts: Roles. Artifacts. All meetings provides a Scrum checklist
- The InfoQ Minibook An Agile Adoption and Transformation Survival Guide includes a checklist for change agents
- Organizational Agile Transformation by LeadingAgile
- Agile Maturity Self-Assessment Survey by Eduardo Ribeiro
- Implementing Lean Software Development (Poppendieck)
- Xebia essentials (free app)

- XebiaLabs DevOps Self-Assessment
- Teammetrics by Christiaan Verwijs
- Agile Assessment by Piotr Nowinski
- Assess your agile engineering practices by Corinna Baldauf
- Agile Maturity Model by Jez Humble and Rolf Russell
- Maturity Assessment Model for Scrum Teams by Marmamula Prashanth Kumar
- The Joel Test: 12 Steps to Better Code by Joel Spolsky
- Back-of-a-Napkin Agile Assessment by Elisabeth Hendrickson
- Are you really agile? by People10
- Process Goals from Disciplined Agile (submitted by Scott W.Ambler)
- Scrum Master Checklist by Michael James
- Top 20 self assessment questions by Gene Gendel
- Project Approach Questionaire by Agile Business Consortium
- Visual Management Self-Assessment by Ben Hogan (free subscription required)
- Lean Agile Intelligence by Michael McCalla (free tool, registration required)
- Continuous Delivery Maturity Checklist by DZone
- The Agendashift(tm) values-based delivery assessment by Mike Burrows (commercial service with free mini edition)
- Retropoly by Sorin Sfirlogea and Florian Georgescu
- How Agile Are You? by Mark Balbes
- quick self-assessment of your organization's agility by Signet / Charles Parry
- Agile Software Development Complete Self-Assessment (paid service)
- DevOps Self-Assessment by Microsoft in collaboration with DevOps Research and Assessment (DORA) - Registration required
- Health Monitors from the Atlassian Team Playbook
- Kanban Service Maturity Assessment by Gerard Chiva

- fluent@agile game by Peter Antman and Christian Vikström
- Agile Alert by H&Z
- Team Agility Self Assessment by Yodiz
- SAFe Team Agility Self-Assessment by Scaled Agile
- Agile Software Product Line Automotive - Assessment Model (aspla) by Philipp Hohl
- Business Agility Manifesto - Diagnostics by Roger T. Burlton, Ronald G. Ross & John A. Zachman
- Agile Assessment by AgileTrailblazers (paid service)
- Enterprise Business Agility Maturity Assessment by Eduardo Ribeiro

If you want to become agile in an agile way, and would like some support on applying any combination of these tools, see my services and diensten, and feel free to contact me!

# Nederlandstalige Agile Assessments

- Agile Zelfevaluatie kaarten door Ben Linders
- Agile Self Assessment door Mike Hoogveld/Nyenrode Business University (Nederlandstalig)

# Background Information on Agile Self-Assessments

The articles and books mentioned below can help you to do agile self-assessment or to develop your own assessment:

- How Agile Are You? on LinkedIn
- Agile Addresses "The Five Dysfunctions of a Team" from InfoQ
- Drexler/Sibbet Team Performance Model
- **Personality types:** Myers-Briggs Type Indicator and DISC assessment
- **Team Dynamics:** Satir Change Model, Human Dynamics and Tuckman's Stages of Team Formation
- Measuring and managing agile maturity (tag: measurement) by Brad Murphy
- Something agile: new ideas for agile implementation by Jan Gentsch
- A List of Agility Tests by David Koontz
- Agendashift by Mike Burrows
- Agile Managen door Mike Hoogveld
- Assess Your Team's Scrum Level Using ShuHaRi and the Celebration Grid by Juergen Mohr
- Are You Agile? An Assessment Can Tell You by Joel Bancroft-Connors
- Model for Team Effectiveness based on research by Richard Hackman

# Getting the Agile
# Self-assessment Cards

The exercises and games described in this book can be played using card decks from the Agile Self-assessment Game.

This chapter provides information about downloading card decks from my webshop or buying packages with the cards and the book.

The Agile Self-assessment Game and all Expansion Packs are licensed under a CC BY-NC-ND 3.0 License. If you want to use the game commercially, please contact Ben Linders.

# Download from Ben Linders' Webshop

The cards from the basic game and all expansion packs can be downloaded in PDF format in my webshop.

 Before buying cards, register your book to buy card decks with a discount coupon at benlinders.com/agile-self-assessment-game.

Available card decks:

- Main Agile Cards
- Scrum Expansion Pack
- DevOps Expansion Pack
- Busines Agility Expansion Pack
- Kanban Expansion Pack

There are also Agile Self-assessment Card decks available in multiple languages:

- Agile Self-assessment Game - English
- Juego Autoevaluación Ágil - Spanish Edition
- Agilní sebehodnotící hra - Czech edition
- Gra Agile Self-Assessment - Polish edition
- Agile Zelfevaluatie Kaarten - Dutch edition
- Jeu de cartes d'autoévaluation Agile - French edition

# Packages with Cards

If you got this book through Leanpub you may have chosen to buy a package that includes cards. Multiple languages are supported with specific packages, currently available are:

- Agile Self-assessment Game - English edition: The book (in English) with 52 basic Agile cards and expansions packs for Scrum (39 cards), Kanban (52 cards), DevOps (26 cards) and Business Agility (26 cards). Total of 195 English cards!
- Juego Autoevaluación Ágil - Spanish edition: The book (in English) with 52 basic Agile cards in Spanish and expansions packs in Spanish for Scrum (39 cards), Kanban (52 cards), DevOps (26 cards) and Business Agility (26 cards). Total of 195 Spanish cards!
- Agilní sebehodnotící hra - Czech edition: The book (in English) with 52 basic Agile cards in Czech and expansions packs in Czech for Scrum (39 cards), Kanban (52 cards), DevOps (26 cards) and Business Agility (26 cards). Total of 195 Czech cards!
- Gra Agile Self-Assessment - Polish edition: The book (in English) with 52 basic Agile cards in Polish and expansions packs in Polish for Scrum (39 cards), DevOps (26 cards) and Business Agility (26 cards). Total of 143 Polish cards!
- Agile Zelfevaluatie Kaarten - Dutch edition: The book (in English) with 52 basic Agile cards in Dutch and expansions packs in Dutch for Scrum (39 cards), Kanban (52 cards), and DevOps (26 cards). Total of 169 Dutch cards!
- Jeu de cartes d'autoévaluation Agile - French edition: The book (in English) with 52 basic Agile cards in French. Total of 52 French cards!

Find more information about the above packages (book and cards) here.

# Training and Support

There are several ways to get trained in playing the game: Take a one-hour kick-off training or buy the corporate edition which includes this training, or attend a public or in-house workshop.

I provide many services for assessing your agility and can help you to increase delivered value.

I want you to be successful. Hence, I provide Free Lifetime Support on everything that I do to help you using what I deliver it in your specific situation.

# Kick-off Training for Agile Self-assessment Game

The kick-off training is a one-hour instructor-led remote workshop to play the Agile Self-assessment Game: Learn how to create the cards, prepare a game and play it with your teams.

After buying this service you will be contacted by me to plan the training and arrange everything. I'm normally available on short notice and am flexible regarding the time to accommodate what works for you.

The kick-off training can be extended to go deeper into the game and gamification. We can turn into a mini-workshop if you want to explore how to use this game as a tool for continuous improvement. Contact me and we'll work it out :-).

This workshop is part of my remote coaching services. These remote services are provided using a video + audio connection (Skype or likewise) at a time that works for you and me.

 My remote workshops and coaching sessions are highly interactive, you'll learn things that you can apply directly in your daily work in a short timeframe without any traveling.

# Agile Self-assessment Game - Corporate Edition

With the corporate edition of the game, organizations can discover how agile their teams are and what they can do to increase their agility to deliver more value to their customers and stakeholders.

The corporate edition of this successful agile game includes:

- Cards for playing the Agile Self-assessment Game
- Expansion Packs for Scrum, DevOps, Kanban, and Business Agility
- Playing Suggestions and Experience Stories
- Multi-team corporate license or up to ten facilitators
- One hour of free remote kick-off training on the game
- Free Lifetime Support

The corporate edition grants the company a license to have the game played within the company by multiple facilitators.

After buying this corporate edition you will be contacted by me to plan the kick-off training and arrange everything. I'm normally available on short notice and am flexible regarding the time to accommodate what works for you.

# Assessing your Agility Services

I provide many services for assessing your agility and can help you to increase delivered value.

The following services are offered:

- In-house workshop: Playing the Agile Self-assessment Game (contact me for details)
- Public workshops which include the Agile Self-assessment Game
- Agile assessment for your team, department, or organization (contact me for details)
- Train the assessors, remote or on-site training for facilitating self-assessments (see also the Kick-off Training mentioned earlier)
- Facilitation for playing the game at your event (conference, meetup, hackathon, game lab, etc)
- Tailoring the Agile Self-assessment Game to your specific needs
- Licenses for playing the game

As a senior adviser and coach with more than thirty years of experience in software development and management, I'm there to guide you through your agile journey and help you increase your agility to deliver more value to your customers and stakeholders.

For the latest information about my services, visit Assessing your Agility.

# Increasing your Agility Workshops

I regularly provide workshops, masterclasses, and training sessions, where people gain new insights, try out different practices and techniques, and learn how to apply them effectively in their own specific situation.

Below find some of the workshops that I give. For up to date information, visit workshops.

**Making Agile Work for You**

If your agile transformation is not delivering results, if you are doing agile and want to deliver more value to your customers and stakeholders: join my workshop Making Agile Work for You.

In this workshop, you will learn how to apply agile practices to develop the right products, deliver faster, increase quality, and become a happy high-performing team!

**Improving Organizational Agility**

If your organization is trying to adopt agile but finding it hard to do that, having difficulties adjusting to short delivery times, and unable to remove barriers that are blocking cross-organizational collaboration: join my workshop Improving Organizational Agility.

Learn how to apply agile throughout your organization by changing the culture and mindset and improve in small but meaningful steps.

**Valuable Agile Retrospectives**

In the Workshop Valuable Agile Retrospectives for Teams you will practice different kinds of retrospective and learn how to adopt and apply retrospectives in your own organization.

# Free Lifetime Support for Playing the Game

I provide Free Lifetime Support on everything that I do to help you using what I deliver it in your specific situation. I want you to be successful.

I will help you to apply things that you learned in my workshops or advisory or coaching sessions, support you if there are questions while or after reading my books, preparing or playing games, or when using any other product or service provided by me.

It works like this:

- Sent me an email and describe your needs. Please include additional information about what you are aiming at and why, the current situation, or anything else that might be relevant.
- I will give you suggestions and/or ideas for what you can do. Normally I will answer within 24 hours.

The reason I do this is that I want the people that I work with and anyone who buys the books that I wrote or games that I created to be successful.

As a buyer and reader of this book, you are entitled to Free Lifetime Support. Please contact me by email at benlinders@gmail.com.

Free Lifetime Support is offered by me with a fair use policy. Play it nice, and I will help you, anytime.

# About the Author

Ben Linders: Trainer / Coach / Adviser / Author / Speaker

*Ben Linders* is an Independent Consultant in Agile, Lean, Quality and Continuous Improvement, based in The Netherlands.

Author of Getting Value out of Agile Retrospectives, Waardevolle Agile Retrospectives, What Drives Quality, and Continuous Improvement. Creator of the Agile Self-assessment Game.

As adviser, coach, and trainer, I help organizations deploying effective software development and management practices. I focus on continuous improvement, collaboration, communication, and professional development, to deliver business value to customers.

I'm an active member of networks on Agile, Lean, and Quality, and a well-known speaker and author.

I share my experiences in a bilingual blog (Dutch and English), as an editor for Culture and Methods at InfoQ, and as an expert in communities like Computable, Quora, DZone, and TechTarget.

Follow me on twitter: @BenLinders.

# Bibliography

**My Blog and Books**

Ben Linders - Sharing my Experience - www.benlinders.com

Getting Value out of Agile Retrospectives - A Toolbox of Retrospective Exercise

What Drives Quality - A Deep Dive into Software Quality with Practical Solutions for Delivering High-Quality Products

The Agile Self-assessment Game - The Agile Coaching Tool For Improving Your Agility

Continuous Improvement - A toolbox for Scrum masters and Agile Coaches to increase agility

Register your book at benlinders.com/agile-self-assessment-game

**Books (Ordered on Title)**

Accelerate by Nicole Forsgren, Jez Humble, and Gene Kim

Agendashift Part 1 by Mike Burrows.

Agile Software Development Complete Self-Assessment Guide by Gerardus Blokdyk.

Debugging Teams by Brian W. Fitzpatrick and Ben Collins-Sussman.

Getting Value out of Agile Retrospectives by Luis Gonçalves and Ben Linders.

iTeam: Putting the 'I' Back into Team by William E. Perry.

Liftoff by Diana Larsen and Ainsley Nies.

Managing for Happiness by Jurgen Appelo.

## Links

Manifesto for Agile Software Development

Agile Self-assessment Game

Agile Self-assessment Tools and Checklists

Assessing your Agility

Agile Coaching Tools

Agile Games Webshop